Natalie,

We have enjoyed hearing your stories, keep up the good work! Enjoy our "trail".

In Golden Fun,

Megan.

Brody + Tehya

Dedicated to all the children that have read with Brody and Tehya.

Brody

the

Reading Tutor

Written and Illustrated by Megan Bell

"Hello Brody! Welcome to Jones Elementary School today."
said Mrs. Gill from behind the office desk.

"The first graders are so happy you are here to listen to their stories."

Miss Megan, Brody's owner, clips the visitors badge on her jacket and straightens his red therapy dog bandana.

B rody started dog school when he was very little, this taught him to walk right next to Miss Megan in the school hallways.

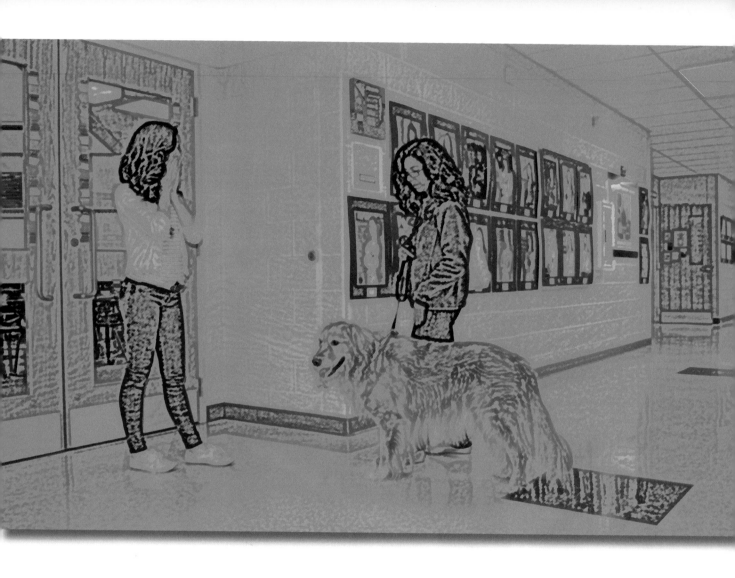

As Brody walks down the hall a child comes out of the library but quickly stops. Miss Megan asks her, "Are you afraid of dogs?"

The girl answers,
"Yes, my mom
tells me all dogs are
mean and dirty, so
I don't like them.
But your dog doesn't
look mean or dirty."
Brody looks up
at her with his big,
dark, puppy dog eyes.

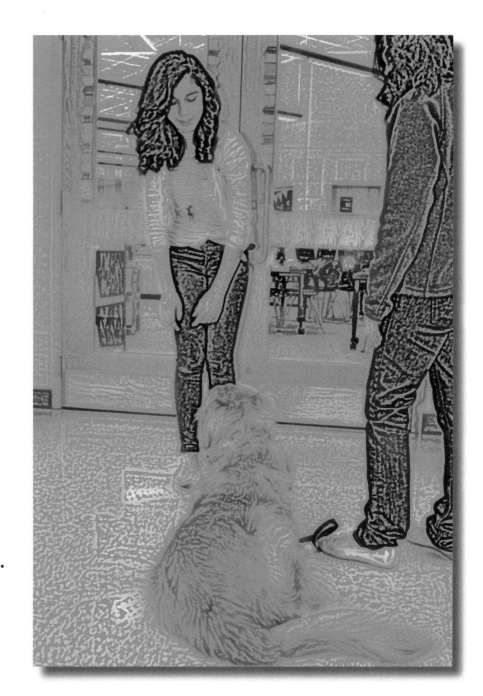

Miss Megan explains the best way to approach a new dog is calmly, with your hand up for a sniff. If you are afraid stand still, big, and wrap your hands on your chest like a tree trunk.

The new dog will usually sniff you and leave you alone until help arrives.

❝**NEVER RUN**, because even the best behaved dog might think you are playing a game of chase!" Miss Megan continues. The girl lets Brody sniff her hand and gives him a pat on the head before heading back to her classroom.

Miss Megan spreads a blanket on the floor for Brody as the first reader, Lydia walks into the room. She has a book about princesses to read today. Brody snuggles right next to her hoping for a fantastic hug!

Matthew comes bopping into the reading room with his football book. Brody's ears perk up when Matthew reads about running and catching balls!

Just as Matthew finishes up; something VERY LOUD buzzes and bright lights flash throughout the school.

It hurts Brody's ears…

B rody, Miss Megan and Matthew quickly follow the others safely out of the building. It is very noisy on the way outside.

The children watch as Brody exits the building. He is very calm and seems to smile at them, letting them know that everything is going to be ok.

Settling back inside the reading room, the next student arrives.

Billy cautiously stands in the doorway. He does not sit on the blanket. He sits across the room in a chair, not even looking Brody's way.

B rody offers his paw, as if introducing himself saying, "Pleased to meet ya!" He rolls upside down and makes funny noises… he is just silly.

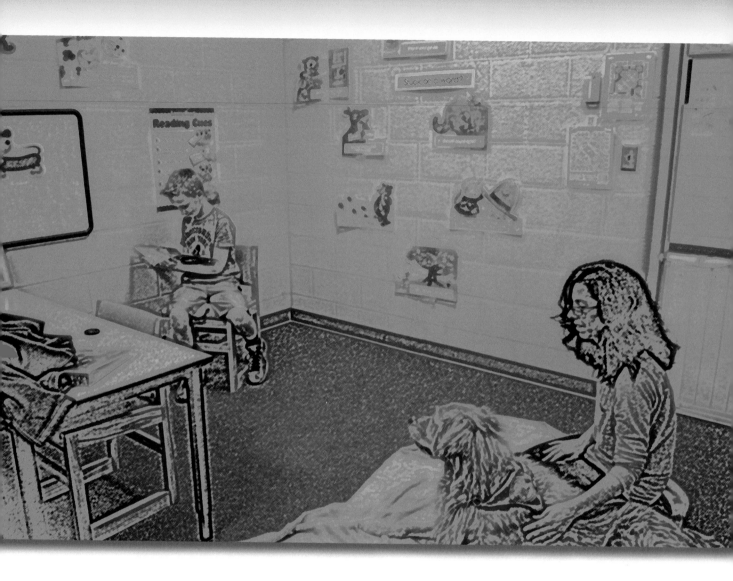

For many visits before this, Brody sat quietly, hoping Billy would come closer. Today he looks at Billy with his big, dark, puppy dog eyes trying to persuade him to sit on the blanket next to him.

It's Brody's lucky day! Billy sits on the blanket and actually holds Brody's paw!

"Pleased to meet ya!" smiles Billy.

"Brody don't fall asleep." Miss Megan giggles. "Oh dear is he snoring too?" Tommy laughs as he finishes reading his book.

He's the last child to read.

Miss Megan starts to clean up and Brody sees some children going outside for recess.

One child drops a ball.

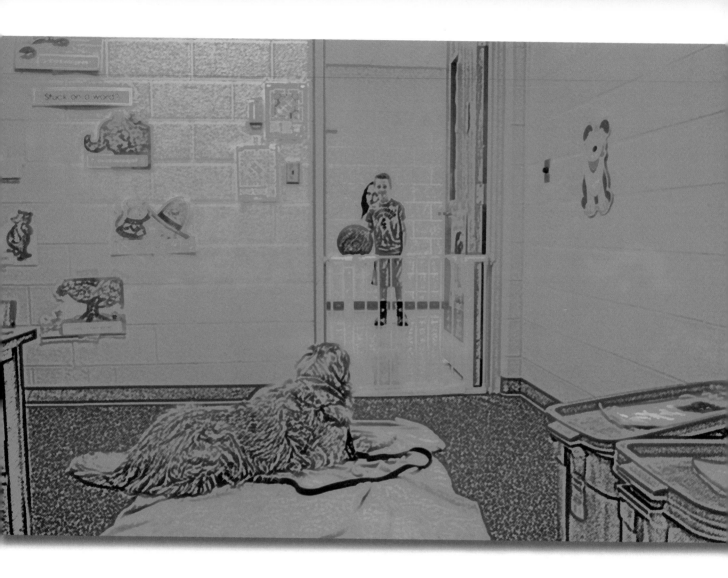

Oh how Brody loves to retrieve balls! But he knows that at school he has to leave it. So he sits and watches as the boy picks up the ball and bounces it outside.

As they leave the school, after another great day of listening to stories, Miss Megan praises Brody!

She tells him, "What good reading tutor you are!" and gives him a treat once they get into their truck.

Off they go until the visit!

E ven if you don't have a dog reading tutor that comes to your school, you can read to your parents, stuffed animals, cat, dog or other pet.

Brody says, "Just grab a book and READ! **WOOF!**"

Fun Facts:

Brody has a sister, Tehya, also a licensed therapy dog.

Brody and Tehya visit many schools throughout Central Ohio.

Brody was born on January 8, 2008.

Theya was born on June 14, 2009.

Brody loves to dock dive and hunt for birds, he is a true athlete.

Tehya is a "Princess", although she competes and wins many awards she likes being a therapy dog the best.

Both are loved and spoiled by their family of four humans.

Brody and Tehya have won many ribbons.

Please visit their website for photos, more information and links at

www.dogreadingtutor.com.

**Brody on his way home at
8 weeks old**

Princess Tehya, 9 weeks old

Brody likes to smile…

Tehya relaxing with a bone.

Keep Reading!

Brody

CPSIA information can be obtained
at www.ICGtesting.com
Printed in the USA
BVIC011948110413
317920BV00003B

* 9 7 8 0 9 8 8 9 7 7 5 0 1 *